Eve,
GET IN
Your
PLACE

Eve, GET IN Your PLACE

Gloria Ward

Christian Living Books, Inc.
An imprint of Pneuma Life Publishing
Largo, MD

Christian Living Books, Inc.
An imprint of Pneuma Life Publishing, Inc.
P.O. Box 7584
Largo, MD 20792
301-218-9092
www.christianlivingbooks.com

ISBN 1-56229-017-7

Printed in the United States of America

Scripture quotations marked (NIV) are taken from the HOLY BIBLE, NEW INTERNATIONAL VERSION®. NIV®. Copyright©1973, 1978, 1984 by International Bible Society. Used by permission of Zondervan. All rights reserved.

Unless otherwise marked, all scripture quotations are taken from the King James Version of the Bible.

DEDICATION

To David

He embraces me with his strength.
He encourages me with his love.
He lifts me high with his faith.
He covers me with his prayers.

At his look, my passions awaken.
At his voice, my heart opens.
At his touch, my body tingles.
At his lips, my love overflows.

He is my friend.
He is my lover.
He is my man.
He is my Husband.

Love always,
Gloria

CONTENTS

ACKNOWLEDGEMENTS

I wish to express my thanks to David, my husband, who has encouraged and supported me in all my endeavors; to my loving and wonderful children: Sharon and Anthony; and to my precious grandchildren: Sharron and Jonathan.

Thanks to Mildred Cox, my mother, for the words of expression on the virtuous wife (Chapter 6).

Thanks to Karen Harrison for her friendship, as well as the invaluable editing, formatting, layout and technical expertise of this book.

Thanks to Helen Johnson for her spiritual insight and constructive critique of the contents and format of this book.

Thanks to Darnell Ward for his guidance and support in the world of modern technology.

Thank you to family and friends for their continued love, patience and support throughout the years.

Most importantly, I thank God who has inspired and taught me from his Word. He has always been with me. He has never forsaken me. Without his love, knowledge and wisdom, this book would not have been possible.

INTRODUCTION

As daughters of Eve, we are definitely out of place – in the workplace, church, home and play. We are continuously manifesting the spirit of mother Eve. **It is not our place to change, control or lead our husbands.** This expression may be difficult to receive. God has authorized the husband's position. If he fails to occupy his position, we do not have legitimate claims to his position. Two objects cannot occupy the same space at the same time. In his infinite wisdom, *God established positions in the home for both the husband and wife*.

In this age of women's rights and equal rights, we have lost sight of our true purpose. My prayer is our eyes will see, our ears will hear and our hearts will receive what the Spirit is saying. The truth will set us free.

When my husband said, "I do," he did not have a clue as to what a strong-willed and independent person he had taken as his wife for life! I was born into a family of bold and determined women who gave me love, inspiration and wisdom as a

1

young child through my adults years. My mother, grandmother and great-grandmother have been awesome role models. They nurtured my strong independent qualities, and thus, the lesson of submission has come hard for me.

During the process of "getting into my place," I concluded that independent thinking and making our own decisions are not negative qualities. God give us all a measure of wisdom and knowledge accompanied by self-will. However, we must not think independent of God or ignore the opinions or contributions of others. The expression "either my way or the highway" will not work in a marriage. The wife as well as the husband must submit to authority.

Submission is NOT bowing to your husband — for there is only one true God. It is not giving up your thoughts and knowledge in terms of "who you are" or "what you know." But it is important to acknowledge that God has given the husband the leadership and responsibilities of the home.

> *But I would have you know, that the head of every man is Christ; and the head of the woman is the man; and the head of Christ is God.* (1 Corinthians 11:3)

God did not create man to rule over the woman, or the woman to rule over the man.

> *And God said, Let us make man in our image, after our likeness: and let THEM have dominion over the fish of the sea, and over the fowl of the air, and over the cattle, and over all the earth, and over every creeping thing that creepeth upon the earth.*

> *So God created man in his own image, in the image of God he created them; male and female created he them.*

And God blessed them, and God said unto THEM, Be fruitful, and multiply, and replenish the earth, and subdue it: and have dominion over the fowl of the air, and over every living thing that moveth upon the earth.
(Genesis 1:26-28)

They (both male and female) were to replenish the earth, subdue it and have dominion over every creeping thing, <u>not each other</u>.

God said that it was not good for man to be alone so He made him a help meet. From Adam's rib, he made woman. God looked upon them as **one, not equal.** The two were **one** flesh, not **equal** flesh.

And Adam said, This is now bone of my bones, and flesh of my flesh: she shall be called Woman, because she was taken out of Man. Therefore shall a man leave his father and his mother, and shall cleave unto his wife: and they shall be one flesh. (Genesis 2:23-24)

Jesus tells us again:

And said, For this cause shall a man leave father and mother, and shall cleave to his wife: and they twain shall be one flesh? Wherefore, they are no more twain, but one flesh. What therefore God hath joined together, let not man put asunder. (Matthew 19:5-6)

Adam and Eve were made to function in a perfect union. In the process of exercising free will, they allowed a third party to divide their union. As a result of sin and disobedience, there was a break in communication between the spirit of man and the Spirit of God. Man/woman became exposed and at the mercy of their own fallen nature and spiritual wickedness. They had fallen into a state of chaos, darkness and confusion.

For God is not the author of confusion, but of peace, as in all churches of the saints. (1 Corinthians 14:33)

He is a God of design and structure. He made every thing to function in decency and order. To establish order in the midst of man's fall from grace, God placed into existence spiritual and natural laws that would require man's subjection and accountability to authority as well as to one another.

It is not always easy to admit wrongdoing. Adam and Eve played the "Blame Game." Today, we face the consequences of their sins.

Unto the woman he said, I will greatly multiply thy sorrow and thy conception; in sorrow thou shalt bring forth children; and thy desire shall be to thy husband, and he shall rule over thee. And unto Adam he said, Because thou hast hearkened unto the voice of thy wife, and hast eaten of the tree, of which I commanded thee, saying, Thou shalt not eat of it: cursed is the ground for thy sake; in sorrow shalt thou eat of it all the days of thy life; (Genesis 3:16-17)

As a consequence of Eve's sin, husbands now have the rule over their wives.

Wives, submit yourselves unto your own husbands, as unto the Lord. (Ephesians 5:22)

He never said that it would be easy. However, if we are obedient to God and submit to our husbands as unto the Lord, we will reap marital bliss, joy, peace and happiness.

The Spirit of the Lord has led me to be frank and honest with myself as well as to you, the reader. **We women must be told**. The truth will set us free. At times we can be stubborn and "half-knowing." No one can tell us what we think we already know. To keep the peace, our husband generally keeps silent and do not always tell us about our "out of place selves." As you read this book, examine your hearts. Do not play the "Blame Game." Point the finger inward – look within yourself.

In writing this book, I do not admit I have all the answers. I am not a licensed marriage counselor, minister, psychologist, psychiatrist or social worker. My experience is based on over thirty-two years of marriage and heeding the continuous teaching and leading of the Holy Spirit. I recognize that each marriage is unique, and each circumstance varies. Therefore, my prayer is that you will allow the Holy Spirit to teach and guide you in all areas of your relationship. Ask the Lord Jesus to open up your understanding. Pray for God's wisdom, knowledge and purpose for your marriage as well as your life, as you read these pages.

Chapter 1

A HAPPY HOME

In the beginning, the Creator provided the First Lady with all of the makings of a happy home.

GOD made and gave her a husband.

> *So God created man in his own image, in the image of God created he him. And the Lord God said, It is not good that the man should be alone; I will make him an help meet for him. And the rib, which the Lord God had taken from man, made he a woman, and brought her unto the man.* (Genesis 1:27; 2:18; 22)

GOD provided and placed them in a home.

Genesis tells us about the home:

> *And the Lord God planted a garden eastward in Eden; and there he put the man whom he had formed. And out of the ground made the Lord God to grow every tree that is pleasant to the sight, and good for food; the tree*

of life also in the midst of the garden, and the tree of knowledge of good and evil. And a river went out of Eden to water the garden; and from thence it was parted, and became into four heads. The name of the first is Pison: that is it which compasseth the whole land of Havilah, where there is gold; And the gold of that land is good: there is bdellium and the onyx stone. And the name of the second river is Gihon: the same is it that compasseth the whole land of Ethiopia. And the name of the third river is Hiddekel: that is it which goeth toward the east of Assyria. And the fourth river is Euphrates. (Genesis 2:8-14)

GOD gave her husband a job.

And the Lord God took the man, and put him into the garden of Eden to dress it and to keep it. And out of the ground the Lord God formed every beast of the field, and every fowl of the air; and brought them unto Adam to see what he would call them: and whatsoever Adam called every living creature, that was the name thereof. And Adam gave names to all cattle, and to the fowl of the air, and to every beast of the field.
(Genesis 2:15; 19-20)

GOD blessed them and brought forth abundant blessings.

And God blessed them, and God said unto them, Be fruitful, and multiply and replenish the earth, and subdue it: and have dominion over the fish of the sea, and over the fowl of the air, and over every living thing that moveth upon the earth. And God saw very thing that he had made, and, behold, it was very good.
(Genesis 1:28; 31)

8

GOD provided nourishing food for the home.

And God said, Behold, I have given you every herb bearing seed, which is upon the face of all the earth, and every tree, in the which is the fruit of a tree yielding seed; to you it shall be for meat. And to every beast of the earth, and to every fowl of the air, and to every thing that creepeth upon the earth, wherein there is life, I have given every green herb for meat: and it was so.
(Genesis 1:29-30)

GOD gave them eternal life.

*And the Lord God formed man of the dust of the ground, and breathed into his nostrils the breath of life; and man became a living soul. And out of the ground made the Lord God to grow every tree that is pleasant to the sight, and good for food; **the tree of life** also in the midst of the garden...* (Genesis 2:7; 9)

From the scripture, it appears as if Adam and Eve's home was in order. Husband and wife are living together in their beautiful home prepared by the Almighty God.

"Eve, Get in Your Place" may be unwelcome words to our ears. At her address on Eden Street, Eve was in her place. She was the "help meet" for her man. God spoke and the land appeared. He put the sun, moon and stars in the heavens. At his command, the waters, streams, trees, plants, and flowers sprang forth. He spoke and the fish of the sea, animals on land, and birds of the air came into being.

He made man and prepared for him a garden to live and work in. He made woman – she was one with her man – bone of his bones and flesh of his flesh. God purposed everything before He made the woman. God prepared husband, home, food, flowers, and everything before she was even made.

Let's look at our marriages of today. Is everything in place for the "Eves" of today? Have provisions of shelter, food and clothing been made?

We dream of a knight in shining armor who comes to sweep us off our feet. We get married and live in a house with a white picket fence and flowers. We raise our children and live happily ever after.

Is this not the dream that little girls have been having forever? It WAS reality and not fantasy for Mother Eve. God prepared her a home with beautiful flowers and trees. He blessed her with a husband made in His image and likeness. Everything was perfect for her.

Eve was bamboozled, lied to, and tricked out of her happy home. Her reality world turned into a nightmare. Are we yet living that same nightmare today? A deceptive third party convinced her that what she already possessed was not enough. The evil one's purpose was to misrepresent the truth, bring division between man and wife, wreck the relationship, and destroy their happy home as well as the homes of all mankind.

Chapter 2

THE THIRD PARTY

God is the founder of the institution of marriage. It was designed to form a permanent union between man and woman. As Father, He presented the bride to Adam. He proclaimed them man and wife. Genesis 1:28 tell us that He blessed them and encouraged them to be fruitful, multiply and replenish the earth. The newlyweds began marriage in a positive direction.

So the couple was enjoying each other. The home was full of love and peace. It was like heaven on earth. An evil visitor entered the garden.

Now the serpent was more subtil than any beast of the field which the Lord God had made. And he said unto the woman, Yea, hath God said, Ye shall not eat of every tree of the garden? But of the fruit of the tree which is in the midst of the garden, God hath said, Ye shall not eat of it, neither shall ye touch it, lest ye die. And the serpent said unto the woman, Ye shall not sure-

ly die: For God doth know that in the day ye eat there-
of, then your eyes shall be opened, and ye shall be as
gods, knowing good and evil.And when the woman
saw that the tree was good for food, and that it was
pleasant to the eyes, and a tree to be desired to make
one wise, she took of the fruit thereof, and did eat, and
gave also unto her husband with her; and he did eat.

(Genesis 3:1-6)

The honeymoon was over. Eve opened her home to this deceptive charmer. She accepted the lies. She allowed a third party to upset her paradise on earth.

In Genesis 2:16-17, God had given the command not to eat from this tree to Adam. Did Adam bring to Eve's remembrance what God had said? Did he hesitantly eat of the fruit of the tree? Did he disobey his God to **keep the peace?**

Is it possible that Eve did not listen to her husband? Yes. She was an active participant in the demise and destruction of her happy home. She allowed a third party to disrupt their happy, loving and peaceful marital relations.

We see how the third party disguised as a serpent destroyed Eve's happy home. Can you discern the third party in your relationship? Does the intruder enter through a friend, family member, job or other outside interests? Women BEWARE of the **arrows of the third party** – the gossiping, the half-truths and outright lies. The grass may look greener on the other side. The third party's motive is to eradicate what you already possess.

John 10:10 tells us the intentions of the third party who visited Eve.

The thief cometh not, but for to steal, and to kill, and
to destroy...

What are some of the tactics of the third party?

1. **Deception: it may look or taste good, but it is not always good for you.**

Eve saw that the tree was good to eat and pleasant to the eye. Apparently, she lacked foresight of the consequences of eating from the tree – expulsion from her happy home and eventually death and destruction for this first family as well as the entire human race. The consequences of her act continue to this day.

2. **Deception presents you with an alternative that is inconsistent with God's word. It sounds good but is not what God has intended for your life.**

> *And Sarai said unto Abram, Behold now, the Lord hath restrained me from bearing: I pray thee, go in unto my maid; it may be that I may obtain children by her. And Abram hearkened to the voice of Sarai.*
> (Genesis 16:2)

Sarai presented an option to Abram. God had told Abram His plan. But Abram chose to listen to his wife. They stepped out of God's plan for them. Sarai's actions opened the door for confusion in her home; there has been lasting tension and unholy wars existing to the present day due to her actions.

3. **Deception saturates your mind with the cares of friends, church, jobs, and the world so that you fail to cherish what God has given you: a husband, children and home.**

Lot's family was told by the angels:

> *Escape for thy life; look not behind thee, neither stay thou in all the plain; escape to the mountain, lest thou*

be consumed. Then the Lord rained upon Sodom and upon Gomorrah brimstone and fire from the Lord out of heaven; And he overthrew those cities, and all the plain, and all the inhabitants of the cities, and that which grew upon the ground. But his wife looked back from behind him, and she became a pillar of salt.
(Genesis 19:17; 24-26)

Apparently, Mrs. Lot's heart was back with her possessions, friends and the other cares or interests that she had left behind. Mrs. Lot lost her most precious possessions – her life and her family.

4. **Deception presents temptations, thus allowing the intruder access into our minds through the doorways of our ears and eyes.**

II Samuel tells us about the temptations of King David.

And it came to pass in an eveningtide, that David arose from off his bed, and walked upon the roof of the king's house: and from the roof he saw a woman washing herself; and the woman was very beautiful to look upon. And David sent and enquired after the woman. And one said, Is not this Bathsheba, the daughter of Eliam, the wife of the Uriah the Hittite? And David sent messengers, and took her; and she came in unto him, and he lay with her; for she was purified from her uncleanness: and she returned unto her house. And the woman conceived, and sent and told David, and said, I am with child. (II Samuel 11: 2-5)

In II Samuel 11:6-13, David attempts to cover-up the sin that he and Bathsheba have committed. He sends for her husband Uriah and tells him to go to his house to be with his wife. Uriah, being a good soldier, sleeps at the door of the King's house and remains with the other servants. Next David attempts to get Uriah drunk and sends him home to sleep with Bathsheba. But Uriah went to lie on his bed with the servants of his lord and did not go to his house to be with his wife.

The story continues in chapter 11:

And it came to pass in the morning, that David wrote a letter to Joab, and sent it by the hand of Uriah. And he wrote in the letter, saying, Set ye Uriah in the fore-front of the hottest battle, and retire ye from him, that he may be smitten, and die. And the shooters shot from off the wall upon thy servants; .....and thy servant Uriah the Hittite is dead also. And when the wife of Uriah heard that Uriah her husband was dead, she mourned for her husband. And when the mourning was past, David sent and fetched her to his house, and she became his wife, and bare him a son...
(II Samuel 11:14-15; 24; 26-27)

King David committed the sin of adultery with his heart and eyes on top of the roof. Failing to resist the temptation, he sent for Bathsheba and yielded to the lusts of the flesh.

There hath no temptation taken you but such as is common to man: but God is faithful, who will not suffer you to be tempted above that ye are able; but will with the temptation also make a way to escape, that ye may be able to bear it. (1 Corinthians 10:13)

The tempter tries everyone. Seducing spirits go to and fro seeking admission to our minds. Our carnal flesh desires the

ungodly pleasures of the world. God will make a way of escape.
Will you resist the temptation? The choice is yours. Genesis
39:12 tells us of Joseph's response to temptation:

> *And she caught him by his garment, saying, Lie with
> me: and he left his garment in her hand, and fled, and
> got him out.*

5. **Deception leads you into circumstances that may result
   in the hardening of hearts one to another.**

   For example, many marriages suffer due to lack of communication. This results in the failure to hear or understand one
another. Hearts become callous. Love waxes cold. Sensitive and
affectionate feelings diminish towards each other. What was
Jesus' response to the Pharisees?

> *They say unto him, Why did Moses then command to
> give a writing of divorcement, and to put her away? He
> saith unto them, Moses because of the hardness of your
> hearts suffered you to put away your wives: but from
> the beginning it was not so.* (Matthew 19:7-8)

Hebrews addresses the hardened heart:

> *Take heed, brethren, lest there be in any of you an evil
> heart of unbelief, in departing from the living God.
> But exhort one another daily, while it is called To day;
> lest any of you be hardened through the deceitfulness of
> sin. For we are made partakers of Christ, if we hold the
> beginning of our confidence stedfast unto the end;
> While it is said, To day, if ye will hear his voice, hard-
> en not your hearts, as in the provocation.*
> (Hebrews 3:12-15)

Hardened hearts bring about the absence of a loving relationship, hindrances in prayer, and lack of blessings.

Seeing ye have purified your souls in obeying the truth through the Spirit unto unfeigned love of the brethren, see that ye love one another with a pure heart fervently. Likewise, ye husbands, dwell with them according to knowledge, giving honour unto the wife, as unto the weaker vessel, and as being heirs together of the grace of life; that your prayers be not hindered. For the eyes of the Lord are over the righteous, and his ears are open unto their prayers: but the face of the Lord is against them that do evil. (1 Peter 1:22; 3:7,12)

Do not allow the third party to sow discord in your relationship. Do not allow the intruder to bring worldly distractions, diverse temptations, or hardened hearts to your home. Do not allow this thief to steal your blessings. He cannot enter the relationship unless you open the door. Ask the Holy Spirit for wisdom and guidance in all areas of your relationship. Jesus watches and hears your prayers. Come together **as one** to help each other. Love one another.

…For this cause shall a man leave father and mother, and shall cleave to his wife: and they twain shall be one flesh? Wherefore they are no more twain, but one flesh. What therefore God hath joined together, let not man put asunder. (Matthew 19:5-6)

God's design for marriage is that twain become one, **not the thrice become one.**

Chapter 3

FALLEN OUT OF PLACE

The fall of man began with the bewitching of Eve and the disobedience of Adam. The evil spirits of confusion and separation reared their ugly heads. Originally God made Adam's physical body as "giver" and Eve's physical body as "receiver." Eve took the fruit and gave it to Adam. Adam took the fruit as well and then assumed the role of receiver. During this exchange, they **reversed roles**. Eve gave Adam the fruit, and he received it. Thus, the fall from their rightful positions began.

Eve's action, which was based on lies, and Adam's disobedience to God's command allowed the spirit of division to enter their home. Created with free will, they both fell prey to their own selfish desires, and this resulted in expulsion from their happy home. Their dream house had turned into a nightmare. Family relations became burdensome and difficult. There was a broken link in the chain of command. The spiritual flow of communication from God to man had been interrupted. Man and woman had "fallen out of place."

If you perceive in your mind that your husband is out of place, you do not have claim to *his position*. In Genesis 3:6: **Eve saw that the fruit was good for food and pleasant to the eyes.**

It is not always what we perceive in our minds. We should ask the Holy Spirit for discernment. Reliance upon one's own perception may lead to deception.

God gave Adam and Eve dominion over the earth and its inhabitants. Adam was the caretaker of the garden. God put him in charge. If your husband is not operating in his rightful place, do not make a move on his position. The Lord will provide for your need (Philippians 4:19). Ask Him to fulfill that position until He leads your husband into his rightful place.

> *For thy Maker is thine husband; the Lord of hosts is his name; and thy Redeemer the Holy One of Israel; The God of the whole earth shall he be called. For the Lord hath called thee as a woman forsaken and grieved in spirit, and a wife of youth, when thou wast refused saith thy God…. And all thy children shall be taught of the Lord; and great shall be the peace of thy children.*
> (Isaiah 54:5;13)

For many years, I was ignorant of the "**in my place**" principle. Obedience to any man other than my earthly father and Lord was definitely out of character. In my carnal mind, I drew the line between submission and obedience. Submission based on my interpretation was compromising "a little bit" on small issues. In contrast, obedience was that "one does not have a say on anything."

I strongly support the biblical command "children obey your parents." However, I chose to ignore the command "wife submit to your husband." Many of my conversations to the Lord started off as: "I am not going to submit to him unless he submits to you." Of course, I believed to know as much as my husband David. The Lord kept telling me to "submit," but I could always justify why it was impossible.

After years of marriage, division began to settle deep into our relationship. We had come to a crossroad – there was no compromise. An invisible line was drawn – each one retreated to his or her side. Although our marriage appeared to have deteriorated, we still prayed and struggled through the process of becoming one as purposed by God.

We began to "pray" and "play." We became skilled players in what I call the **"Blame Game."** Remember, when approached by God, Adam blamed *that woman*, and Eve blamed *the serpent.*

I would pray, "Lord, he is your child. You must make him do what he is supposed to do – I am trying."

David would pray, "Jesus, you gave me this woman, now you have to fix her because I cannot do anything with her, and I am in my place."

So there we were – Jesus was the referee as well as the judge.

Whenever a disagreement arose, he would say: "Eve, get in your place." With my closed mind and hardened heart, I stopped listening to him. **I did not hear him address me as "Eve."**

One day, while visiting a local church, I noticed women who were in every possible leadership position: pastor, worship leader, deacons and ushers. In my mind, there were about three "mousy" looking men in the entire congregation. **Note: One's perception can lead to deception.** The women appeared to be in control.

The worship and praise service was in full swing. I was in the Spirit, and I felt His presence all around me. In a gentle and peaceful voice, I heard Him speak: **"Eve get in your place."** I opened my eyes and looked around the church, again observing women operating in every leading role – "it made sense to me." The Holy Spirit spoke a second time: **"Eve get in your place."** I became uneasy and began to struggle with what I should do. The thought of telling the women in the church to "get in their place" was frightening. The Holy Spirit spoke a third time: **"Eve, Get in your place."**

My response to the Holy Spirit was "I cannot tell these women to get in their place. They will throw me out of this church."

Joy and bliss immediately left me. Fear replaced confidence. Guilt and shame became partners with fear. I had disobeyed the command of God. To ease my conscience, I told myself that I would ask for forgiveness in a few days for not being obedient. To lift my wounded spirit, I convinced myself that I would soon be back in the good graces and fellowship of the Holy Spirit.

A few weeks passed. I had asked for forgiveness and believed the incident to be in my past. While washing dishes, the Holy Spirit spoke again, **"Eve, Get In Your Place."** I responded immediately: "Oh! You were talking to me – OKAY."

Immediately, I knew that he was speaking to me, not the women in the church. I did not question or dispute the command, but instead totally yielded to the Holy Spirit. The prospects of submission to David seem easier than telling my sisters in the church that "they" were out of place.

After twenty years of marriage, Gloria finally **got the message**. At that moment, the process of submission and **getting**

into my place began. David had submitted to Jesus. Our house was now in order. There was spiritual communication with our Lord. We began to receive answers to prayers. The blessings were overflowing. We began to operate in God's purposed plan for marriage.

Chapter 4

THE PURPOSED EVE

There are many women manifesting the spirit of Eve in the workplace, home, church and play. **We do not know our purpose. We have lost our way. We are out of our place. As time goes on, the Eve nature gets even more out of whack.** We continue to be bamboozled by the third party.

In contradiction to women's rights – man and wife were to become **one and not equal**. God presented Eve wonderfully made to fulfill Adam's natural being.

Where is our place? What is our purpose?

God purposed women's position as follows:

- to complement the man – **not** be the man
- to be taken care of – **not** take care of the man
- to be virtuous Godly women – **not** simulated "supermen"
- to be our husband's glory – **not** be his image of shame
- to be the sole bearers of the seed – **not** be the sole supporters

Eve, GET IN *Your* PLACE

1. Women were created to complement him.

*And the rib, which the Lord God had taken from man,
made he a woman, and brought her unto the man.*
(Genesis 2:22)

God gave Adam his bride as the complete and finishing touch of his creation. They were to fulfill each other's natural desires and needs.

2. Women were created to be taken care of.

The husband is to love and provide for his wife. He is not to neglect or abuse her. Ephesians 5:33 tells the husband to *love his wife as himself.* She is God's daughter. The wife is not the provider – **it is the job of the husband.** *She is there to work with him, not without him.* When the woman moves into the position of provider, she has strayed from her purpose.

3. Women were created to be virtuous Godly women.

We are not men; therefore, we should not be in place of a man. We may feel that we do not need our husbands to do for us. We may believe that we can do it ourselves. But when we seek to take on the roles of men, we become angry, bitter, dissatisfied, stressed, tired, unhappy and wrinkled complainers. As our husbands take their positions, and we get into our places, we reap the attributes of a Godly woman – blessed, chaste, discreet, faithful, honest, meek, quiet spirit and wise.

4. Women were created for our husband's glory.

For a man indeed ought not to cover his head, foras-much as he is the image and glory of God: but the woman is the glory of the man. (1 Corinthians 11:7)

As wives, we mirror our husband's character. Our treatment in the home will reflect outside the home. Will we glorify or image his shame?

> *A virtuous woman is a crown to her husband: but she that maketh ashamed is as rottenness in his bones.*
> (Proverbs 12:4)

Ephesians 5:25 tells husbands to love their wives as Christ loves the church. Follow the example of His love and care for the church – the roadmap that leads to a "happy home."

5. Women were created as sole bearers of the seed.

> *And Adam called his wife's name Eve; because she was the mother of all living.* (Genesis 3:20)

> *I will therefore that the younger women marry, bear children, guide the house, give none occasion to the adversary to speak reproachfully.* (1 Timothy 5:14)

> *My son, hear the instruction of thy father, and forsake not the law of thy mother.* (Proverbs 1:8)

> *And, ye fathers, provoke not your children to wrath: but bring them up in the nurture and admonition of the Lord.* (Ephesians 6:4)

> *For the children ought not to lay up for the parents, but the parents for the children.* (2 Corinthians 12:14)

God holds both parents responsible for the rearing of the children. Although the woman carries the child in the womb, she is the mother, not the father. Both roles are equally important and essential to the well being of the child. If one is absent, you must ask and rely on the Holy Father to occupy the missing position.

In search of God's plan for my life, I believed I knew my place and purpose in my marriage. David had spoken the words many times to my deaf ears – "Eve, get in your place." I did not hear him. When the Holy Spirit first spoke in church, it was obvious to me the "other" women were out of place.

When the Holy Spirit spoke to me in the kitchen "Eve, Get in your place," I immediately knew that He was talking me.

My husband prayed faithfully for help with his wife. God had revealed to him the divine purpose and order of our marriage. He knew he had to get into place and submit to Lord Jesus Christ as his head. In obedience, he took back his position. However, through the Holy Spirit, he "discerned" his wife was out of place and infringing on his position. By this point we had stopped trying to change the Adam and Eve-like nature in each other and had turned each other over to God. It was then we realized it was not our place to change each other. **Only God can do it – that is His place.**

If you do not know the purpose for your marriage, the entire family suffers. Love, peace, and happiness fleeth, while sorrow, confusion and frustrations lieth at the door. If you are not in your place, **your purposed partner may begin seeking his or her purpose in all the wrong places.**

Chapter 5

THE FALLEN ADAM

I n search of our Adam, we at times have gone ahead of God. We have made wrong choices for our mates. Our man may be guided by his sinful carnal nature and is not subject to the Spirit of God. He rejects the headship of our Lord Jesus Christ. He leads the home in his way– which can result in an ungodly rule over the home.

Based on decisions of the heart, you may find yourself in unfavorable conditions. You take on depression, stress, tensions and burdens that you were not intended to bear. As you seek God for relief in your circumstances, the following questions may need to be answered: *Who or what joined you together? Did you seek God for this individual? Was it love? Was it lust? What bondage have you brought upon yourself as well as your children?*

While you continue to honestly view your current environment, further "what if" questions may arise. Always remember that regardless of the problems, **Jesus is Lord**. He is always in

29

control. As your read the following "what if's" proclaim **GOD IS!!!!**.

1. What if he fails to provide?

- He fails.

  But if any provide not for his own, and specially for those of his own house, he hath denied the faith, and is worse than an infidel. (1 Timothy 5:8)

- God never fails!!!

  Philippians assures us:

  But my God shall supply all your need according to his riches in glory by Christ Jesus. (Philippians 4:19)

2. What if he will not work?

- He does not?

  This we commanded you, that if any would not work, neither should he eat. (2 Thessalonians 3:10)

  Proverbs 14:23; 18:9; and 21:25 continue:

  All work brings a profit, but mere talk leads only to poverty. (Proverbs 14:23 NIV)

  One who is slack in his work is brother to one who destroys. (Proverbs 18:9 NIV)

  The sluggard's cravings will be the death of him because his hands refuse to work. (Proverbs 21:25 NIV)

He who has been stealing must steal no longer, but must work, doing something useful with his own hands, that he may have something to share with those in need. (Ephesians 4:28 NIV)

- God will!!!

  Two are better than one; because they have a good reward for their labour. (Ecclesiastes 4:9; 5:19)

  Every man also to whom God hath given riches and wealth, and hath given him power to eat thereof, and to take his portion, and to rejoice in his labour; this is the gift of God. (Ecclesiastes 5:19)

12:14 says:

  He becometh poor that dealeth with a slack hand: but the hand of the diligent maketh rich. (Proverbs 10:4)

  A man shall be satisfied with good by the fruit of his mouth: and the recompence of a man's hands shall be rendered unto him. (Proverbs 12:14)

3. What if he is ignorant of God's purpose for his life?

- He lacks knowledge?

  Proverbs 29:18 and Matthew 15:14 tell us:

  Where there is no vision, the people perish: but he that keepeth the law, happy is he.

  Let them alone: they be blind leaders of the blind. And if the blind lead the blind, both shall fall into the ditch.

- <u>God is omniscient!!!</u>

These scriptures speak of our powerful God who knows all things:

> *In the beginning was the Word, and the Word was with God, and the Word was God. The same was in the beginning with God. ll things were made by him; and without him was not any thing made that was made.*
> (John 1:1-3)

> *I am Alpha and Omega, the beginning and the ending, saith the Lord, which is, and which was, and which is to come, the Almighty.* (Revelation 1:8)

Proverbs advises us:

> *Trust in the Lord with all thine heart; and lean not unto thine own understanding. In all thy ways acknowledge him, and he shall direct thy paths.*
> (Proverbs 3:5-6)

4. What if he is abusive?

- <u>Third party's plan.</u>

> *Be sober, be vigilant; because your adversary the devil, as a roaring lion, walketh about, seeking whom he may devour.* (I Peter 5:8)

> *The thief cometh not, but for to steal, and to kill, and to destroy:* (John 10:10)

- God's plan!!!

  > ....*I am come that they may have life, and that they may have it more abundantly.* (John 10:10)

  > *Husbands, love your wives, and be not bitter against them.* (Colossians 3:19)

  > *So ought men to love their wives as their own bodies. He that loveth his wife loveth himself. For no man ever yet hated his own flesh; but nourisheth and cherisheth it, even as the Lord the church.* (Ephesians 5:28-29)

  > *Live joyfully with the wife whom thou lovest all the days of the life of thy vanity, which he hath given thee under the sun, all the days of thy vanity: for that is thy portion in this life, and in thy labour which thou takest under the sun. Whatsoever thy hand findeth to do, do it with thy might; for there is no work, nor device, nor knowledge, nor wisdom, in the grave, whither thou goest.* (Ecclesiastes 9:9-10)

  > *Make no friendship with an angry man; and with a furious man thou shalt not go; Lest thou learn his ways, and get a snare to thy soul.* (Proverbs 22:24-25)

5. **What if he fails to participate in the rearing of the children?**

- Man does not.

  > *But if any provide not for his own, and specially for those of his own house, he hath denied the faith, and is worse than an infidel.* (1 Timothy 5:8)

33

And whosoever shall offend one of these little ones that believe in me, it is better for him that a millstone were hanged about his neck, and he were cast into the sea.
(Mark 9:42)

Behold, the third time I am ready to come to you; and I will not be burdensome to you: for I seek not yours, but you: for the children ought not to lay up for the parents, but the parents for the children.
(2 Corinthians 12:14)

- God shall!!!

    There is help for the fatherless:

    And all thy children shall be taught of the Lord; and great shall be the peace of thy children. (Isaiah 54:13)

    Thou are the helper of the fatherless. (Psalm 10:14)

    Sing unto God, sing praises to his name: extol him that rideth upon the heavens by his name JAH, and rejoice before him. A father of the fatherless, and a judge of the widows, is God in his holy habitation. (Psalm 68:4-5)

    To visit the fatherless and widows in their affliction
    (James 1:27)

6. What if he is an unbeliever?

- Before you say I do, God has said!!!

    The apostle Paul tells the single women and men:

    Be ye not unequally yoked together with unbelievers: for what fellowship hath righteousness with unrighteousness? and what communion hath light with dark-

*ness? And what concord hath Christ with Belial? Or
what part hath he that believeth with an infidel? And
what agreement hath the temple of God with idols? for
ye are the temple of the living God; as God hath said,
I will dwell in them, and walk in them; and I will be
their God, and they shall be my people. Wherefore come
out from among them, and be ye separate, saith the
Lord, and touch not the unclean thing; and I will
receive you, And will be a Father unto you, and ye
shall be my sons and daughters, saith the Lord
Almighty.* (2 Corinthians 6:14-18)

• <u>Oops! You have already said I do.</u>

To the married believers, the scriptures say this:

*And unto the married I command, yet not I, but the
Lord, Let not the wife depart from her husband: But
and if she depart, let her remain unmarried, or be rec-
onciled to her husband: and let not the husband put
away his wife.* (1 Corinthians 7:10-11)

To married believers who are unequally yoked:

*But to the rest speak I, not the Lord: If any brother
hath a wife that believeth not, and she be pleased to
dwell with him, let him not put her away. And the
woman which hath an husband that believeth not,
and if he be pleased to dwell with her, let her not leave
him. For the unbelieving husband is sanctified by the
wife, and the unbelieving wife is sanctified by husband: else were your children unclean; but now are
they holy. But if the unbelieving depart, let him depart.
A brother or sister is not under bondage in such cases:
but God hath called us to peace. For what knowest*

*thou, O wife, whether thou shalt save thy husband? or
how knowest thou, O man, whether thou shalt save thy
wife?* (1 Corinthians 7:12-16)

7. What if he is an adulterer or a whoremonger?

• He commits adultery.

Thou shalt not commit adultery. (Exodus 20:14)

*Confidence in an unfaithful man in time of trouble is
like a broken tooth, and a foot out of joint.*
(Proverbs 25:19)

*Can a man take fire in his bosom, and his clothes not
be burned? Can one go upon hot coals, and his feet not
be burned? So he that goeth in to his neighbor's wife;
whosoever toucheth her shall not be innocent. Men do
not despise a thief, if he steal to satisfy his soul when he
is hungry; But if he be found, he shall restore sevenfold;
he shall give all the substance of his house. But whoso
committeth adultery with a woman lacketh understanding: he that doeth it destroyeth his own soul. A
wound and dishonour shall he get; and his reproach
shall not be wiped away.* (Proverbs 6:27-33)

*Whoso loveth wisdom rejoiceth his father: but he that
keepeth company with harlots spendeth his substance.*
(Proverbs 29:3)

• God's Purpose!!!

*Marriage is honourable in all, and the bed undefiled:
but whoremongers and adulterers God will judge.*
(Hebrews 13:4)

God's plan for marriage was not divorce. In the beginning it was not so. He intended for marriage to be a permanent union. Matthew 19:6 tells us: **what God hath joined together, let not man put asunder.** We make a covenant in marriage to love, honor and obey. We promise to be faithful and love one another. When we fail to keep our commitment, we break the covenant. When we commit adultery, we break the bond of unity and oneness.

Adultery is not restricted to committing the act. Jesus tells us:

> *That whosoever looketh on a woman to lust after her hath committed adultery with her already in his heart.*
> (Matthew 5:28)

These adulterous thoughts are the root cause of marital infidelity. You must not dwell on these ungodly thoughts, but think on the wonderful blessings your heavenly father has provided for you. Is it worth the risk, to lose it all for a brief lustful moment?

The Word enlightens us on three causes of marital separation: death, sexual immorality, and being unequally yoked. Signs of spiritual and physical deterioration of a marriage, with the exception of death, may be a cold heart, bitterness, failed love, and non-communication. These seeds of destruction can lie dormant in the relationship for years, until it finally destroys the marriage.

1. Death: The spirit leaves the body resulting in physical death.

Paul tells the church:

For the woman which hath an husband is bound by the law to her husband so long as he liveth; but if the husband be dead, she is loosed from the law of her husband. So then if, while her husband liveth, she be married to another man, she shall be called an adulteress: but if her husband be dead, she is free from that law; so that she is no adulteress, though she be married to another man. (Romans 7:2-3)

The wife is bound by the law as long as her husband liveth; but if her husband be dead, she is at liberty to be married to whom she will; only in the Lord.
(1 Corinthians 7:39)

2. **Sexual Immorality: Engaging in spiritual and physical sexual relations with someone other than the marital partner may eventually lead to divorce.**

Jesus speaks to us on adultery and divorce:

It hath been said, Whosoever shall put away his wife, saving for the cause of fornication, causeth her to commit adultery: and whosoever shall marry her that is divorced committeth adultery. (Matthew 5:31-32)

The Pharisees also came unto him, tempting him, and saying unto him, Is it lawful for a man to put away his wife for every cause? He saith unto them, Moses because of the hardness of your hearts suffered you to put away your wives: but from the beginning it was not so. And I say unto you, Whosoever shall put away his wife, except it be for fornication, and shall marry another, committeth adultery: and whoso marrieth her which is put away doth commit adultery. (Matthew 19:3, 8-9)

In the NIV read as follows:

*But I tell you that anyone who divorces his wife, except for **marital unfaithfulness**, causes her to become an adulteress, and anyone who marries the divorced woman commits adultery.* (Matthew 5:32 NIV)

*I tell you that anyone who divorces his wife, except for **marital unfaithfulness**, and marries another commits adultery.* (Matthew 19:9 NIV)

3. Unequally Yoked:

I am of the belief that God did not put some marriages together. He had nothing to do with it. You stepped out on your own, and did not wait on Him. In some marriages, you made your vows with a person who was unbelieving, under-achieving, unloving, and uninteresting. What does light have to do with darkness? James 3:11 asks Doth a fountain send forth at the same place **sweet** water and **bitter**? There is a spiritual disconnect from the beginning. You both leave the altar going forward in different directions.

Paul speaks of a remedy for the unequally yoked:

...If any brother hath a wife that believeth not, and she be pleased to dwell with him, let him not put her away. And the woman which hath an husband that believeth not, and if he be pleased to dwell with her, let her not leave him. For the unbelieving husband is sanctified by the wife, and the unbelieving wife is sanctified by the husband: else were your children unclean; but now are they holy. But if the unbelieving depart, let him depart. A brother or a sister is not under bondage in such cases: but God hath called us to peace.
(1 Corinthians 7:12-15)

If there is unfaithfulness in your marriage, pray and seek wisdom from the Lord. Ask the Holy Spirit to direct your steps. Allow God's Word to shine light into darkness; seek His peace in confusion, and pray His angels to provide safety in danger.

There may be other "what if's" in your relationship not discussed in this chapter. However **Jesus is Lord**. He is still in control. Submit yourself to your husband as you submit unto the Lord. He will lead and direct every step you take. Trust Him with your circumstance. Jesus is the head of every man – even your fallen Adam. Fast and pray for his salvation. 1 Peter 3:1-2 tells us: **Likewise, ye wives, be in subjection to your own husbands; that, if any obey not the word, they also may without the word be won by the conversation of the wives; While they behold your chaste conversation coupled with fear.**

An early commitment in <u>my</u> marriage to this principle would have resulted in marital bliss sooner and not later. In order for the communication and blessings of God to flow freely – this must take place or else you live with the "what if" circumstances in your relationship.

Chapter 6

THE HELP MEET

G od purposed Eve for Adam. She was there to help him care for the garden – not care for it by herself.

- **We are not the providers, but the "receivers" of the provisions.**

- **We are not the covering, but are to be covered.**

- **We are not the leaders, but essential assistants.**

- **We are not in charge, but have a significant input.**

- **We are not the final word, but have an important say.**

God saw that it was not good that Adam was alone. He took a part of Adam and made a helpmeet suitable for him. Eve was bone of his bones and flesh of his flesh (Genesis 2:22-23). She was wonderfully made to make him happy and complete. This wonderful creation is "Woman."

Who is this Godly woman? Where is this "suitable" woman today? How can we find her? In Proverbs 31, King Lemuel was in search of such a wife. He looked to his mother for guidance. The King's mother's illustrious instructions to her son became the testimonial of the attributes of a wife throughout the ages:

Who can find a virtuous woman? for her price is far above rubies. The heart of her husband doth safely trust in her, so that he shall have no need of spoil. She will do him good and not evil all the days of her life. She seeketh wool, and flax, and worketh willingly with her hands. She is like the merchants' ships; she bringeth her food from afar. She riseth also while it is yet night, and giveth meat to her household, and a portion to her maidens. She considereth a field, and buyeth it: with the fruit of her hands she planteth a vineyard. She girdeth her loins with strength, and strengthen her arms. She perceiveth that her merchandise is good: her candle goeth not out by night. She layeth her hands to the spindle, and her hands hold the distaff. She stretcheth out her hand to the poor; yea, she reached forth her hands to the needy. She is not afraid of the snow for her household: for all her household are clothed with scarlet. She maketh herself coverings of tapestry; her clothing is silk and purple. Her husband is known in the gates, when he sitteth among the elders of the land. She maketh fine linen and selleth it; and delivereth girdles unto the merchant. Strength and honour are her clothing; and she shall rejoice in time to come. She openeth her mouth with wisdom; and in her tongue is the law of kindness. She looketh well to the ways of her household, and eateth not the bread of idleness. Her children arise up, and call her blessed; her husband also, and he praiseth her. Many daughters have done virtuously, but thou excellest them all. Favour is deceitful, and beauty is vain: but a woman that feareth the Lord, she shall be praised. Give her the fruit of her hands; and let her own works praise her in the gates. (Proverbs 31:10-31)

Praise the name of our Lord Jesus Christ! What exquisite jewels we find in these verses. The King's mother provides such wonderful attributes of a virtuous wife.

Like King Lemuel, I have been blessed with a godly mother. Her life as a virtuous mother and wife has been a beautiful example for me to follow. It is only fitting that I present to you the following words of expression from my mother, Mildred Cox, on Proverbs 31:

The thirty-first chapter of Proverbs is a conversation between King Lemuel and his beloved mother. I am not sure at what time in his life the conversation took place. It may be that the King was seeking a wife. It possibly may be an exchange from a mother to her son as he matures and becomes groomed to begin his life on the throne of Israel. She gives him sage of wisdom on many, many things that he will face in life. However, we find that this mother was also instructing her son on the qualities of a wife that would make him happy as well as complete.

Verse 10: Who can find a virtuous woman?

This question lets us know that this adventure in **search** of a wife is not to be taken lightly. Proverbs 18:22 tells us *"Whoso findeth a wife findeth a good thing, and obtaineth favour of the Lord."* **Her price is far above rubies.** We know in our present time, rubies are expensive, but not unattainable.

V. 11: Safely trust in her.

Truthful: All the husband's trust in his wife brings peace to his mind. He can only think good of her because she will be open and honest in her exchange with him and everyone around her.

V. 12: She will do him good and not evil all the days of her life.

Honorable: The heart's desire of his wife will be to honor, esteem, and not to destroy him.

V. 13: Seeketh wool, and flax,...worketh well with her hands.

Fruitful: She will look and find ways to make her husband and children enjoy their home and surroundings. The works of her hands are abundantly blessed.

V. 14: Like the merchants' ships.

A go-getter: She will go near and far to help bring goods or food to her family. She will till the ground, tend the livestock or sell wares at the market for the good of her family.

V. 15: She riseth also while it is yet night.

Early riser: She will be the first to rise from slumber at the early hour to start taking care of her household.

V. 16: She considereth a field and purchases it.

Knowledgeable and wise: She thinks about what is good for the family. In agreement with her husband, she realizes a good business venture and with resources obtained by her own hands, she buys a vineyard; plants and cultivates it for her household.

V. 17: Girdeth her loins....strengtheneth her arms.

Bold and strong: She prepares herself mentally and spiritually for the tasks that are given her as woman, wife and mother. Her arms are strengthened. She holds all things dear to her heart and performs her tasks with love as she trusts in the Lord.

V. 18: Her lamp goeth not out by night.

Faithful: She believes in the position that has been given to her. She approaches her endeavors with knowledge that marriage is honorable by God. She keeps in mind that being faithful and vigorous honors her God, husband and children.

V. 19: Layeth her hands to the spindle....hold the distaff.

Vigilant of her household: She is always careful for her household. Work is no hardship where her family is concerned. She will put self in the background for the good of her family. She will be ever watchful for her husband and family.

V. 20: Stretcheth out her hands.

Helping hands: It is a joy for her to help those in need. She reaches beyond herself to help the poor. She helps in words as well as deed. Wherever the need, you will find her fingerprints.

V. 21: Not afraid of the snow.

Adversity adapter: She is not afraid of what time brings. She adapts to the seasons on behalf of her family. She strives and aims high for her loved ones.

V. 22: Maketh herself.

Self-love as well as love for others: She is aware that in order to give love and care to others, she must care for and love herself. She is secure and happy in her God given place. She loves herself because she is comfortable in the love of her husband and God. As she strives to be the vessel who loves and cares for her household, she adorns herself with the fine things of beauty. Her inward virtues of tenderness, compassion, patience and long-suffering are all appealing to her husband's eyes.

V. 23: Her husband is known in the gates.

Lighthouse for her husband: She honors and presents her husband in the best light to all mankind. She understands that they are one and her actions, as well as words, speak to who her husband is.

V. 24: Maketh fine linen; selleth; and delivereth.

Woman: Her goals are always on behalf of her husband and household. She continues to strive to keep the standards high for the good of the unit as a whole. She maketh, selleth and delivereth it. **She knows how to get the job done.**

V. 25: Strength and honor are her clothing.

Clothed in the righteousness of the Lord: She has learned to rest in the Lord Jesus and put on His righteousness. There will be good times and bad times. Through it all, she relies on His strength. She knows that **joy** will come.

V. 26: Openeth her mouth with wisdom...her tongue is the law of kindness.

Godly wisdom: She is ever seeking knowledge for her position. She speaks with wisdom. She tries to deal with the problems that come her way with solutions for the good of others who are placed in her path. She provides thoughtful advice through kindness and love.

V. 27: Looketh well to ways of her household....bread of idleness.

Watchful. She stays the course that has been set before her. She is diligent about her household. She is ever on guard for their welfare. She tries not to waste a frivolous moment. Her time must be put to good use in everything. She loves life, and desires to be cheerful, joyful, happy, charming and all those wonderful things that bring peace and contentment to life.

V. 28: Children call her blessed....husband praiseth her.

Blessed: The children and husband praise her. In her labor of love of being a wife and mother, this blessed woman is going in the right direction. Her husband is praising his finding of her. The children are thankful because she is much more than someone who birth them, but a mother in all that she does or says.

V. 29: Many daughters have done virtuously.

The Rare Gem: There are many wives that have done virtuously. There are many diamonds, but only one "hope diamond." It is used as a measurement for all diamonds. This verse applies to the wife, mother and woman in the Proverbs "Thou excellest all." All wives have the opportunity to excel. Like the hope diamond, the characteristics of the virtuous wife can be an apex to reach for or far exceed.

V. 30: Favor is deceitful, beauty is vain ...feareth the Lord.

Godly beauty: Earthly favor is very shallow. Only the favor of the Lord God is everlasting. Today, one may have the favor of mankind. Tomorrow, the same person may be despised. Beauty is transient - it keeps you forever trying to maintain it because it will in time fade away. Only that beauty which comes from within will last. A woman who reverences God is a woman who shall be praised.

V. 31: Give her the fruit of her hands.

Honor her: Give her praise for what she has accomplished with her own hands and intellect. Praise her motherhood, sisterhood and womanhood. Value her work in the home, neighborhood, workplace, school, church and all the earth. Praise and honor her for what she has done.

Dear daughters, when we stand and agree to become his mate in marriage, we then become wives. King Lemuel's mother was giving him the pattern of a godly wife who with time becomes the virtuous wife. It is not an overnight event. Like the "hope diamond," the greatest value is hidden inside the stone. It takes chipping, cutting, shaping, grinding and polishing to evolve into a beautiful stone that many have given all their money and sometimes lives to obtain.

We, too, can become virtuous wives. The road has been paved by many that have come before us. God has wonderfully made us for this powerful position of help meet. Proverbs 18:22 proclaims, "Whoso findeth a wife, findeth a good thing."

— Mildred Cox

Chapter 7

THE COVERING

In Genesis 3:7-11, Adam and Eve realized they were naked. Their eyes were opened and fear came upon them. They no longer felt the protection of their God. Adam and Eve had come from under the divine covering of God. They sewed fig leaves together to make themselves coverings. In the cool of the day, they heard the voice of the Lord walking in the garden. They both attempted to hide themselves from his presence amongst the trees. God said: "Where are you?" Adam answered that he was naked and so he hid. God said to Adam, "Who told you that you were naked? Have you eaten of the fruit of the tree that I commanded you not to?"

Life in the Adam's family had changed. In the beginning, there was love, peace, unity and happiness in the marriage. Then division, distrust and criticism moved on the scene. Pleasant appearances to the eyes, now had become distorted. They looked upon each other's nakedness and saw each other's faults. They immediately sought to cover-up instead of taking full responsibility for their wrongdoing. Knowledge of evil, sense of guilt, and feelings of shame came with their loss of innocence.

> *Hast thou eaten of the tree, whereof I commanded thee that thou shouldest not eat? And the man said, The woman whom thou gavest to be with me, she gave me of the tree, and I did eat. And the Lord said unto the woman, What is this that thou hast done? And the woman said, The serpent beguiled me, and I did eat.*
> (Genesis 3:11-13)

Adam and Eve failed to repent of their actions. They played the "Blame Game" and continued the cover-up. Adam's response to God was, "The woman whom thou gavest to be with me." Was he blaming God as well as his wife? In refusing to protect his wife, he left her to fend for herself. In fending for herself, Eve was tricked, but she, too, failed to accept full responsibility for her actions by blaming the serpent.

The God of Love became the God of Justice. He rendered the judgments for their wrong doings.

> *But of the tree of the knowledge of good and evil, thou shalt not eat of it: for in the day that thou eatest thereof, thou shalt surely die.* (Genesis 2:17)

Death had entered the garden on this very day. The God of Mercy made them coats of skin to cover them. Adam and Eve stepped from under the covering of God to a covering of flesh. They were no longer in the positions that God had designed for them.

However, like Adam and Eve, many have chosen to cover themselves. This self-covering is of the flesh. If the husband or wife is not in submission to God's plan, they fall prey to the works of the flesh. Paul tells us:

> *But I would have you know, that the head of every man is Christ; and head of the woman is the man, and the head of Christ is God.* (1 Corinthians 11:3)

God has provided a divine order for the home. Jesus is the covering for the husband; the husband the covering for the wife, and God covers us all. Under God's cover, one enjoys the grace of the Lord Jesus Christ, and the love of God, and the fellowship of the Holy Spirit.

Do you know which covering your marriage is under? Galatians 5:19-21 tells us of the fruits of the spiritual cover versus the works of the cover of flesh:

SPIRITUAL	FLESH
Love	Hatred, Envyings
Emulation	Murders
Joy	Wrath
Peace	Strife, Sedition
Long-suffering	Variance
Gentleness	Revellings
Meekness	Uncleanness
Goodness	Adultery
Faith	Fornication
Temperance	Lasciviousness
	Idolatry
	Witchcraft
	Heresies
	Drunkenness

Under the spiritual covering, man must follow the example of Jesus' love for his bride, the church. He must love and lead his family. The wife should respect and support his leadership. Thus, they are mutually working together to build a "happy home."

If you are not under the spiritual covering, and the home is symptomatic with all of the works of the flesh, begin to fast and pray for deliverance.

> *And he said unto them, This kind can come forth by nothing, but by prayer and fasting.* (Mark 9:29)

Ask the Holy Spirit for guidance in such circumstances. It may become necessary to depart until such time that the Lord may lead your mate into his or her authorized position or remove him or her from the "happy" home.

Chapter 8

"HE SHALL RULE OVER THEE"

Many sermons and conversations have focused on the pain and suffering of Eve in child bearing. However, we have overlooked the phrase "and he shall rule over thee."

> *Unto the woman he said, I will greatly multiply thy sorrow and thy conception; in sorrow thou shalt bring forth children; and thy desire shall be to thy husband,* ***and he shall rule over thee***. (Genesis 3:16)

In the beginning, God gave Adam and Eve dominion over every creeping beast, *not Adam over Eve*. God equipped us with knowledge, wisdom and free will. Because of Eve's sin, we all fell under the judgment whereby we are subject to our husbands. The scriptures plainly identify and support the positions in the home. God in his infinite wisdom knew that it would be difficult for the woman to submit to her husband. To ease the burden and suffering that may come with bondage, he required a hierarchy of headship. I reiterate again:

> *But I would have you know, that the head of every*
> *man is Christ; and the head of the woman is the man;*
> *and the head of Christ is God.* (1 Corinthians 11:3)

God made man in his image and likeness. However, man
fell into sin and separated himself from the Holy God. The
connection back to God was Jesus. Therefore, man is subject
to the Lord Jesus Christ and the woman subject to her husband as unto the Lord.

> *Likewise, ye wives, be in subjection to your own hus-*
> *bands; that, if any obey not the word, they also may*
> *without the word be won by conversation of the wives;*
> *While they behold your chaste conversation coupled*
> *with fear....Likewise, ye husbands, dwell with them*
> *according to knowledge, giving honour unto the wife,*
> *as unto the weaker vessel, and as being heirs together of*
> *the grace of life; that your prayers be not hindered.*
> (1 Peter 3:1-2; 7)

The transition of the two becoming one is not an easy one
for there is the chipping and scraping away of unhealed scars
and hidden emotional hurt. Walls built will have to come
down. We must renew our minds as well as our vocabulary.
The **me** and **I** must be replaced with the **we** and **us**. If we submit to our appropriate headships, the burden will become
lighter.

Along with the sorrow in conception and bringing forth
children, the desire to our husbands and his rule over us was
the consequence for Eve's wrongdoing. Wives are under the
rule of their husbands. However, we must submit to him as
unto the Lord. The way in which you submit to the Lord Jesus

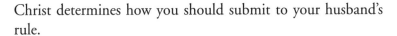

Christ determines how you should submit to your husband's rule.

- Do you submit to the commands of the Lord Jesus Christ grudgingly?

- Do you criticize and complain about what Jesus has provided for you?

- Do you scheme and circumvent events before the Lord to have your own way?

- Do you think you can solve the problems without seeking Jesus for the solution?

- Do you give the Lord Jesus Christ the silent treatment, if He does not respond in the way you want?

I do not believe that we respond to the Lord Jesus Christ in any of the ways mentioned above. We submit to Him in reverence and adoration. We believe Him to be omnipotent, omniscient and omnipresent. We would not imagine acting in such an ugly way to our Lord.

The Lord tells us to submit unto our husbands **as unto Him.** This is the example we must follow. Although God has allowed our husbands the rule over us, He also gave us both free will and the ability to think. We are wonderfully made to achieve and succeed at whatever we set our minds to. Let us honor the authority of our husbands. Let us not respond in a conniving, hateful or revengeful manner towards our husbands. We must strive to dwell with him in love, peace and respect.

55

Chapter 9

SUBMISSION

God performed the first marriage ceremony. He gave away the bride. He pronounced them husband and wife. He blessed them, and the end of their story is written.

What makes a successful marriage? Do these sayings sound familiar? "You must make a commitment. You have to compromise. You should give and take. The marriage should be 50-50. We can do our own thing."

Ephesians 5:22-33 gives three spiritual truths for the husband and wife in the home:

1. Wife **submit** to your husband; and husband **submit** to Jesus as your Head; (2) Husband **love** your wife as Jesus loves the church; and (3) the two would be one.

My response to a successful marriage would be to love, submit, and come together as one. This is consistent with God's divine plan to strengthen and prepare the family to meet the day to day challenges.

Wives, submit yourselves unto your own husbands, as unto the Lord. For the husband is the head of the wife, even as Christ is the head of the church: and he is the saviour of the body. Therefore as the church is subject unto Christ, so let the wives be to their own husbands in every thing. Husbands, love your wives, even as Christ also loved the church, and gave himself for it; That he might sanctify and cleanse it with the washing of water by the word. That he might present it to himself a glorious church, not having spot, or wrinkle, or any such thing; but that it should be holy and without blemish. So ought men to love their wives as their own bodies. He that loveth his wife loveth himself. For no man ever yet hated his own flesh; but nourisheth and cherisheth it, even as the Lord the church. For we are members of his body, of his flesh, and of his bones. For this cause shall a man leave his father and mother, and shall be joined unto his wife, and they two shall be one flesh. This is a great mystery: but I speak concerning Christ and the Church. Nevertheless, let every one of you in particular so love his wife even as himself; and the wife see that she reverence her husband.

(Ephesians 5:22-33)

I learned the lessons of submission later in my marriage. For years I resisted submission to my husband. I knew that to obey the Lord Jesus Christ I had to submit completely. "Allowing" my husband to think that he was in charge was not submission. Deceptive acts and messages on our part will not work. "Wives, submit to your husbands, **as unto the Lord.**" Jesus knows our hearts and intentions. If we practice to deceive our own husbands, are we not deceiving the Lord?

A few years ago, I had to undergo a trial of submission. Without a doubt, I emerged a victor, not a victim.

David was one day out of the hospital recuperating from surgery. He was still under the influence of medication. An incident occurred in which an immediate financial decision had to be made. Since he was not well and under physical pressure with the ongoing medical condition, he refused to discuss the issue. I understood and sympathized with his situation, but I also knew something had to be done. Unable to communicate with him, I went to the Lord.

Based upon my professional experience concerning this matter, I knew what I needed to do. However, the information needed at the time could only be obtained with his permission. *Should I ask him? He's not listening to me. Do I go behind his back? It will only upset him.* I asked the Holy Spirit for guidance.

The role of the "help meet" now came into play. The word "helper" in my mind was the same as to assist, support, take care of or make better. I became the assistant ready to assist. I became the supporter, ready to support. I became the advocate, ready to resolve the problem. Reassured with my role as helper, I stepped out in faith on behalf of my husband as well as myself. I prayed for favor from those whom I was seeking information. The Lord gave me favor, and I received the necessary documentation to resolve the issue.

I informed David a few days later as to what had occurred. He did not appear to be upset, yet commented that it only proves what he had been saying, "I do not listen to my husband."

Did he really mean that I do not obey him? The obedience/submission controversy resurfaced.

Submission meant to "yield to his rightful position as the authority over me." However, submission did not mean that I could not think for myself. I came into the marriage gifted with knowledge, wisdom and my own real-life experiences. I respected my husband's right not to discuss the problem. However, due to his illness, he was not able to act in our best interest. So, I went to Jesus who is my husband's authority.

We are not leaders over our husbands but are joint partners in the marriage relationship. As you both grow spiritually and closer to the Lord, He will lead and guide you step by step. As you operate in your rightful positions, two minds and bodies will emerge as one flesh. You are no longer two going in the opposite direction but are two working as one to build the home in the same direction, pointing upward and giving glory to the Lord.

While writing this chapter, The Holy Spirit gave me the following parable:

Fred and Flo (husband and wife) are going for an afternoon drive. Fred is driving and by Flo's account is going in the wrong direction. Flo knows the highway ends at the edge of a cliff and at Fred's speed soon they will end up at the bottom of the cliff. However, Fred will not heed her warnings and continues to speed toward the wrong direction.

Flo calmly says: "Excuse me, Husband dear. I respect what you believe to be true; however, you are mistaken. Please stop the car. This is where I get off, because I do not want to go over the cliff and die."

Fred stops the car. Flo gets out.

Flo honored Fred's belief as well as his position. She realized he was in error and acted by getting out of the car. From the side of the road, she watched her husband speed toward the cliff and as his "help meet" she prayed that the Lord would send the angels to intervene for both their sakes.

We should imitate Flo. Submit without **going off the cliff.**

1. Submit unto your own husband.

Do not fear or rebel against submission unto your husband. **As the church is subject unto Christ, so are we to be subject to our husbands in everything.** He has instructed the **men to love their wives even as He loved the church and gave himself for it. He sanctifies and cleanses His bride with the washing of water by the Word.**

Jesus has given the example of how wives are to be treated. He is our protection against ungodly rule by our husbands. Our husbands must answer to God for their treatment of God's daughters.

2. Honor your husband.

The scriptures support this principle:

Nevertheless let every one of in particular so love his wife even as himself; and the wife see that she reverence her husband. (Ephesians 5:33)

Except the Lord build the house, they labour in vain that build it. (Psalm 127:1)

You must accept, honor and respect your husband's leadership in your home. Trust in the Lord and rest under His spiritual covering. God knows his strengths and weaknesses. Accept his capabilities as well as limitations. Pray for God's wisdom, knowledge and understanding in his life. Always keep in mind that you both are but clay in the hands of the Potter. (Isaiah 64:8)

3. Recognize The Provider.

The scriptures tells us that providing would become a struggle:

> *And unto Adam he said, Because thou hast hearkened unto the voice of thy wife, and hast eaten of the tree, of which I commanded thee, saying, Thou shalt not eat of it: cursed is the ground for thy sake; in sorrow shalt thou eat of it all the days of thy life; Thorns also and thistles shall it bring forth to thee; and thou shalt eat the herb of the field; In the sweat of thy face shalt thou eat bread, till thou return unto the ground; for out of it wast thou taken: for dust thou art, and unto dust shalt thou return.* (Genesis 3:17-19)

Our husbands are providers, but not The **PROVIDER**. *They were made in the image and likeness of God, but they are not God.* They must provide and maintain food, clothing and shelter for their families. We must consider their human abilities. They are not **super** men, **super** perfect or **super** wealthy.

Every man also to whom God hath given riches and wealth, and hath given him power to eat thereof, and to take his portion, and to rejoice in his labour; this is the gift of God. (Ecclesiastes 5:19)

When you want possessions beyond the basics – a **new** car, **second** house or the thirtieth pair of shoes, consider your man's income. I know all these things are important because we love to receive. However, as help meets, **we are to help**

him, not break him. Only God is almighty, everywhere and knows all things. You both may seek Him for the impossible - not look for the impossible in each other.

4. Know your Purpose.

> *According as He hath chosen us in him before the foundation of the world, that we should be holy and without blame before him in love. Having made known unto us the mystery of his will, according to his good pleasure which he hath purposed in himself:*
>
> (Ephesians 1:4;9)

The Lord spoke to Jeremiah:

> *Before I formed thee in the belly I knew thee; and before thou camest forth out of the womb I sanctified thee, and I ordained thee a prophet unto the nations.*
>
> (Jeremiah 1:5)

The Psalmist David wrote:

> *For thou hast possessed my rein: thou hast covered me in my mother's womb.* (Psalm 139:13)

> *Thus saith the Lord that made thee, and formed thee from the womb, which will help thee; Fear not, O Jacob, my servant; and thou, Jesurun, whom I have chosen. Thus saith the Lord, thy redeemer, and he that formed thee from the womb, I am the Lord that maketh all things; that stretched forth the heavens alone; that spreadeth abroad the earth by myself.*
>
> (Isaiah 44:2; 24)

Praise the Name of Jesus! Praise His Holy name! Praise the sovereignty of our God! He is the supreme ruler of us all. I can place my name in the above scriptures. You can do the same!

He has chosen (place your name) before the foundation of the world. Nothing has happened by chance. He has purposed me for the role of woman, wife and mother. He has blessed me with the knowledge of who I am in Christ. I can step into my rightful position and do the work that God has purposed for me.

5. Be led by the Holy Spirit.

Eve's lust of the eyes and desires of the flesh led to devastating consequences. Manifestations of the fruit of the Spirit and the works of the flesh were outlined in Chapter 7. Adam and Eve stepped from under the spiritual covering. We must allow the Holy Spirit to help bring us under the spiritual covering. Let us walk in the Spirit whereby we will reap the righteous fruits.

Chapter 10

STEPPING INTO PLACE

Before we begin the process of getting into place, we first must realize how we stepped out. It began with Mother Eve's seven steps away from her "happy home."

Step 1. Desiring the forbidden.

Step 2. Listening to the "wrong party."

Step 3. Reversing her role as receiver.

Step 4. Failing to acknowledge wrongdoing - participating in the cover-up.

Step 5. Blaming someone else for her actions.

Step 6. Reaping the consequences of her sins and

Step 7. Being evicted from her "happy home."

Knowledge of where you come from, will **get** you where you're going. Go forward **in the name of Jesus** with the next seven steps to your "happy home."

Step 1. Desire the fruit of the Spirit.

Keep the lines of communication open by allowing love, joy, goodness and peace to continue to flow during the sunshine as well as the rainstorms.

Step 2. Begin to listen to your husband.

Pray for the Spirit of wisdom and knowledge. Ask the Lord to open your ears to hear and your heart to understand.

Step 3. Become the "receiver" and not the "giver."

God made us to receive from our husbands. He made all the provisions available for Eve to receive from Adam. Eve stepped out of place by "giving" the fruit of the tree to Adam. Adam likewise became "receiver" by accepting the fruit. They reversed roles. We need to step into place and begin receiving all the Lord has made available for us through our husbands.

Step 4. Put on the appropriate covering.

In accordance with scripture - our husbands are our covering. No longer our mother, father, sister, brother, friend or neighbor - but our husbands. Our husbands are wonderfully made to be our covering.

God is our overall covering. Know that your husband is the provider, but God is the overall **Provider**. Honor the divine plan of authority. Open up the lines of communication and allow the blessings to flow.

Step 5. Stop the "Blame Game."

Take responsibility for your own actions. If your husband is not operating appropriately in his position, go before Jesus in prayer. Tell him all about it. Remember, Jesus is the head of your husband.

> *But I would have you know, that the head of every man is Christ; and the head of the woman is the man; and the head of Christ is God.* (1 Corinthians 11:3)

God is on the throne and sees everything. He does take care of his daughters.

> *The Lord looketh from heaven; he beholdeth all the sons of men. From the place of his habitation he looketh upon all the inhabitants of the earth. He fashioneth their hearts alike; he considereth all their works.*
> (Psalm 33:13-15)

Step 6. Sow to reap an abundant blessed harvest.

You have heard the expression, "You will reap what you sow."

> *For he that soweth to his flesh shall of the flesh reap corruption; but he that soweth to the Spirit shall of the Spirit reap life everlasting.* (Galatians 6:8)

Allow the Holy Spirit to cultivate your mind and prepare your heart to receive the joy and heavenly benefits of your God-given position. If you sow good seeds, you will reap a blessed harvest.

Step 7. Get stepping.......Step into your "Happy Home"

Let's look at Jeremiah's prayer chapter:

> *LORD, I know that the way of man is not in himself: it is not in man that walketh to direct his steps. O LORD, correct me, but with judgment; not in thine anger, lest thou bring me to nothing.*
> (Jeremiah 10:23-24 NIV)

The Psalmist says:

I have considered my ways and have turned my steps to your statues. I will hasten and not delay to obey your commands. (Psalm 119:59-60)

A simple man believes anything, but a prudent man gives thought to his steps. In his heart a man plans his course, but the Lord determines his steps.
(Proverbs 14:15; 16:9 NIV)

I have chosen to obey the commands of the Lord to step into place. The words of this book were by the inspiration of the Holy Spirit. *It is written as it was given.* It is now up to you as to what you will do. I close with one of my favorite scriptures:

Every wise woman buildeth her house: but the foolish plucketh it down with her hands. (Proverbs 14:1)

ABOUT THE AUTHOR

I was born and raised in West Virginia. Upon graduation from high school, lack of jobs brought me to Washington, D.C. It was love at first sight. As our nation's capitol is such a beautiful city. Seven years later, I married and we raised our family in the suburbs. With over 32 years of marriage under our belts, my husband and I are enjoying the fruits of our labor with family and friends.

I have a Bachelor of Science Degree in Public Accounting from Benjamin Franklin University. I've been in the financial field for over twenty years, providing accounting and consulting services to large and small corporations.

As a young girl, I was gifted with writing poetry. My beloved Pastor requested that I write a poem each Sunday and read it to the congregation. For seven years, with the inspiration of the Holy Spirit, I was in submission to her request. Like a minister seeking the Lord for his/her Sunday message, I would seek the Lord for His wisdom and guidance for each Sunday's poem. He never failed me. It was through this experience that I learned to wait and listen for the voice of the Holy Spirit.

My early works of poetry were destroyed in a fire in the family home. It was truly heartbreaking to loose those poems. They are lost to me forever; however, God remembers every word.

I can remember a couple lines: "In the midst of death, life still goes on…." (inspired while attending a friend's funeral) and "On November 21, 1962, a great tragedy took place… The assassination of a Great Man… that grief-stricken the whole human race…." (This poem about the great John F. Kennedy was read in church and published in my high school newspaper).

Although I have had ups and downs, the Lord has given me favour. The influence of my family and friends as well as my experiences and training have led me to His purpose and plan for my life. I have sought him for direction in my home and work. Having His guidance in the home was a blessing in my marriage.

My husband is a wonderful man of God. Many times we could not, and would not agree. The Lord brought him to the knowledge that he had to submit to his Headship in order for his wife to submit to him. He obeyed the Holy Spirit and submitted to the Lord Jesus Christ as his Head. My husband believing that he was in his place, continued to pray for his wife, (Eve) to get in her place." The fruit of a husband's prayer is recorded forever in heaven and earth.

The Spirit of the Lord moved upon this chosen vessel to birth this book. Through obedience to the Holy Spirit, I wrote it down in a book. I believe it is God's divine roadmap for His sons and daughters to find their way back to His divine plan for the home.

Gloria Ward
P.O. Box 1177
Clinton, MD 20735-1177
www.evegetinyourplace.com